Come 'n Get It

At the Ranch House

B. M. Barss

The recipes have been tested and updated for use in today's kitchens

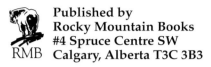
Published by
Rocky Mountain Books
#4 Spruce Centre SW
Calgary, Alberta T3C 3B3

We acknowledge the financial support of the Government of
Canada through the Book Publishing Industry Development
Program (BPIDP) for our publishing activities.

Printed in Canada

ISBN 0-921102-51-8

Cover photo: The kitchen in the MacKay Place Bed &
Breakfast, Millarville, Alberta. Recipes shown in the
photo are Spiced Beef [page 43] Tomato Aspic [page
44], Air Buns [page 21], and Corn Bread [page 17].

Designated an Alberta Historic Resource, the ranch
house was built in 1895 by John and Wilhelmina
Turner, and was known as Balgneggan Stock Farm
after the family farm in Scotland. The stove in the
photo is the original.

In 1902 the ranch was purchased by the Francis
Wright family, and in 1916 by the MacKay family to
whom the present owners are related. Besides running
a thriving Bed & Breakfast operation, the family is
busy restoring the ranch house to its original integrity.
Visitors can view the very first Turner homestead—a
log cabin built in 1886—which still stands in the
grounds.

Our sincere thanks to our host Jacqueline Chalmers.

Photographer: Geoff Williams

CONTENTS

The correct riding attire—a jacket, skirt or trousers, boots, gloves and hat. At the turn of the century, "ladies" rode sidesaddle, both legs on the same side of the English-style saddle.
Photo credit: Glenbow Archives

Introduction

Come 'n Get It at the Ranch House is about ranch homes and kitchens in Western Canada, about the women who occupied them and the food that was prepared in them. It is also about the lifestyle and wonderful hospitality of the ranching community.

Early ranch homes were simple affairs. The first accommodation was often a tent on the ground. In parts of Saskatchewan and Alberta where there were few if any trees, the ranchers lived in sod dwellings made by piling blocks of heavy prairie sod over a log frame. As soon as possible log structures were built, usually a low, two- or three-room house with one door leading outdoors and a window on each side. Along the Whitemud River in Saskatchewan, the log homes were whitewashed with local clay. But in most areas the logs were left to weather with no finish on the outside.

Many interiors were given a light coat of calcimine, which brightened them considerably. In other homes the walls and ceilings were covered with coarse white cotton, which made the interior warmer and brighter. Other interiors were papered with old newspapers to keep out winter drafts.

The log home of the Macleod family in Alberta was well papered with old newspapers during the visit of Lord Lorne. After the prebreakfast morning prayer, Lord Lorne remained on his knees long after everyone else had risen. The Macleods were quite impressed with his devoutness until they realized that he was merely reading an article on the wall that had caught his attention.

In the early days the cooks were men, but as more women came West they eventually took over the task. As the character and size of ranches changed so did the method of working. Women were expected to participate in the running of the ranch, as were the children.

Ranchers butchered their own animals, corned beef, ground sausages, smoked bacon, saved drippings for cooking or making soap, preserved fruit and prepared jam. Large gardens produced vegetables for canning, pickling and storing in the root cellar. Bread, buns, pies and cake were baked at home.

Generally ranch people were thrifty and self reliant. They were proud of their ability to produce and prepare food from their land. They remain so today.

Ranching no longer dominates the Canadian West, but it remains an important industry. Its traditions of simple, gracious living, love of the outdoors, and a spirit of freedom and adventure are revered today. And an appetite for old-fashioned ranch foods remains hearty.

Material for this book has been collected from letters, diaries, manuscripts, history books, family cookbooks and interviews with ranching families. There have been many enjoyable occasions and extraordinary instances of hospitality offered during my research: an invitation sight unseen by the Osbornes to their lovely ranch home nestled near old Fort Walsh; a viewing of Laura Parsonage's private collection of pioneer ranch house artifacts; dinner with Dorothy Blades on an old-fashioned ranch table with a swinging Lazy Susan centre; a day with Bert Sheppard at the OH and an invitation to his eightieth birthday party; a visit with Meriel Hayden; lunch and pemmican at Jean Hoare's and a view of Willow Creek where the bull trains camped overnight a hundred years ago; Fred McKinnon's introduction to his fabulous family; a visit to the Commercial Hotel in Maple Creek; a fall drive through the beautiful Cariboo country.

My sincere thanks to all who provided information and to the helpful staff of the many museums and archives that I visited.

RANCH WOMEN

Ranch women came from all levels of society. There were mail order brides and titled ladies, illiterate housemaids and talented poets. They were plain looking and beautiful, young and old. Whatever their origins and attributes, to survive in the West it was necessary to adapt to the new life and to work hard.

On large ranches their work was generally confined to the house and gardens. On small ranches they participated in all aspects of ranch work. A few led privileged lives, with hired help and a governess for their children. However, in a country where there were at least two men for every woman, it wasn't long before female help was courted and married by a lonely bachelor and the "privileged" woman had to do her own work.

For hard work, consider Mrs. Bennett, who made and sold 108 pounds of butter each week besides attending to other chores, or Marie Rose Smith who tanned leather, made soap, dried meat, preserved berries and gave birth to seventeen children unattended by a doctor.[1]

Mrs. Burke, a young bride from Ireland, lived on a ranch in the foothills, so isolated that she spent one-and-a-half years without seeing another white woman. Looking back, she recalled, "I longed to hear my own name." Once she was alone on the ranch with three small children during a blizzard. Fearful of a chimney fire, she dared not leave them alone. "I couldn't even milk the cow for eight days."[2]

Mrs. Denny with two prairie chickens ready for plucking. Prairie chickens, partridges, ducks, geese and large game were all part of the rancher's menu. Like most ranch women, Mrs. Denny was handy with a gun. c. 1919.
Photo credit: Glenbow Archives

Ranch women loved a good time too! Bea Godden rode a horse sixty miles to Calgary to go to a dance. On a fall day Mrs. Macleay liked nothing better than to hitch her horse to a buggy and drive off to hunt prairie chickens. Mrs. Boulton at Aldersyde sat in her rocker and fished with a willow rod, using grasshoppers for bait. Mrs. Billy Cochrane rode to the hounds with as much vigour as she had back home in England, even though in Canada she had to chase a coyote instead of a fox.

They have left a legacy of pride and independence as strong as that of the men with whom they shared their lives.

Chicken 'n Dumplings

Monica Hopkins attended the Priddis Fair in 1910 and admired the jars of preserved chicken exhibited on the long trestle tables. "They made my mouth water they looked so delicious. I longed to retire to bed and be fed an invalid fare of chicken and fruit."[3]

Serves 6

4 pounds [2 kg] stewing chicken, water to cover

1 medium onion, sliced

2 stalks celery and leaves

1 bay leaf

6 tbsp [100 mL] flour

1/2 cup [125 mL] cream

1 tsp [5 mL] salt

1 tsp [5mL] sage

1/2 tsp [2 mL] thyme

1/8 tsp [1/2 mL] pepper

Cut chicken into serving pieces and place in a large pot. Cover chicken with water. Add the onion, celery and bay leaf. Cover and simmer for 3 hours or until tender.

Remove chicken. Strain and measure broth. There should be approximately 4 cups of broth. If there is more, reduce by boiling; if less, add water. Mix flour with a little cold water to form a smooth paste. Stir into broth and heat until thickened. Add cream, salt, sage, thyme and pepper. Remove the chicken from bones and return meat to gravy.

Prepare dumplings and drop by spoonfuls into hot gravy. Cover and simmer for 20 minutes without removing lid. Serve chicken surrounded by dumplings on a large, deep platter.

Dumplings

1-1/2 cups [375 mL] flour

2 tsp [10 mL] baking powder

3/4 tsp [3 mL] salt

1 egg

1 cup [250 mL] milk

Sift flour, baking powder and salt into a bowl. Mix egg and milk and stir into the dry ingredients. Drop into hot gravy and simmer covered 20 minutes.

THE WEDDING

Mr. and Mrs. Ed Hartt on their wedding day.
Photo credit: Glenbow Archives

"When I was a bride there was no High School or Normal any nearer than Edmonton, and no business opportunities for young women, so after finishing Public School we simply stayed home. We enjoyed many pleasures, however, such as riding, dancing, horseback riding and swimming in the river. There were no discussions about bath houses, or heated pools in those days. Riding sidesaddle over the wide open spaces with thoroughbreds was wonderful. The prairie in spring and summer was covered with long grass, myriads of wild flowers. Indeed it was something to be never forgotten!

There were not many young women in the district but there were several bachelors, so my sisters and I had many admirers. I had one in particular, who rode quite a distance to see me as often as he could. Even in cold weather and through deep snow Lem Sexsmith came to call and always said it was worth it. I was scarcely grown up when my decision was made.

We had quite a large house, and prepared to have the wedding at home, for there was no church in the district. All our friends and neighbours were invited. Miss Janie Suitor, later Mrs. Bob Findley, made my dress and it took quite a while to make. It was cream cashmere trimmed with cream satin and lace, it had large legs of mutton sleeves, and a long sweeping skirt with a dust ruffle. It was lovely!

On the afternoon of the service one long table was set, and as we did not have enough chairs we used benches with homemade quilts, which proved quite comfortable. A neighbour, Mrs. Fred Dowell, was an excellent cook and came to help with the preparations. We had a wedding cake, dozens of custard and dried apple pies, homemade bread and buns, and roast beef.

I doubt if there was a turkey in the whole of southern Alberta at the time.

After the service we visited, had dinner and danced until morning. Our music was supplied by Charlie Shattuck and his fiddle, with various guests taking turns on a mouth organ. As there had been a bad storm that night, all the guests stayed until daybreak so they could see to find their way across the unfenced prairie.

In the morning Lem and I left for our home on the Little Bow, which was the old Samson and Hartford Ranch. We had a good team of horses and a homemade sleigh with blankets and quilts and hot rocks to keep our feet warm. This was our wedding trip, and a wonderful ride it was. To my dismay several guests followed us and because of the heavy storm stayed at our house for a week! What a send-off for a bride!"

Mrs. J. L. Sexsmith recalled: That was the beginning of our happily married life.[4]

Light Fruitcake

This recipe has been used in western Canada since the turn of the century. It is easy to prepare and makes a mild-flavoured fruitcake suitable for weddings, Christmas entertaining, teas and packed lunches.[5]

4 cups [1 L] flour
2 tsp [10 mL] baking powder
1 tsp [5 mL] salt
1 pound [500 g] butter
2 cups [500 mL] sugar
8 eggs
1 pound [500 g] candied citron or extra raisins*
1 pound [500 g] red cherries or dried apricots*
1 pound [500 g] sultana raisins
1/2 pound [250 g] blanched, chopped almonds
2 lemons, juice and grated rind

Sift flour, baking powder and salt. Cream butter; add sugar and beat until light and fluffy. Add eggs, one at a time, beating well after each addition. Combine dried fruits, nuts, lemon rind and lemon juice. Fold the dry ingredients alternately with fruit into creamed mixture.

Prepare two deep 8 inch [20 cm] fruitcake pans or four 4x8 inch [11x20 cm] loaf pans. Line pans with brown paper and grease paper well with butter. Pour mixture into pans. Smooth top of each. Bake at 325° F [160° C] for 15 minutes and then turn oven temperature to 275° F [140° C] for 1-1/2 to 2 hours. The loaf pans will require approximately 1-1/2 to 2 hours; the square pans approximately 2 to 2-1/2 hours. Check doneness by inserting a toothpick. If toothpick comes out dry, cake is done.

* An excellent variation for those who do not care for citron and cherries is to double the amount of sultanas and substitute dried apricots for the cherries. To use apricots, wash and soak for ten minutes, then chop, pour 1/2 cup [125 mL] Cointreau or Brandy over top and leave to soak over night.

A Rangeland Shivaree

The custom of shivareeing a new bride and groom was observed in many ranching communities. The usual procedure was to gather every noisemaking device the group could find. After the newlyweds' lights went out, the fun-makers surrounded the house, banged pots and pans, rang cowbells and fired guns until they were invited inside for a party.

Dancing, card playing and other games would last until the small hours of the morning. The guests always brought lunch—sandwiches, doughnuts and the makings for coffee. Sometimes the fun-makers got carried away, such as the group of cowboys who decided to surprise their newly married friend, a ringleader of many former pranks.

A packed snow drift—a path of easy access to a roof top.
Photo credit: Glenbow Archives

It was winter when the new husband carried his bride over the threshold of their sod-roofed shack. The couple had just settled down for a good night's rest when the wild group of cowboy friends rode up and circled the place on their horses while whooping, hollering and firing guns. One of the riders galloped up a packed snowbank right onto the roof. When the bride and groom looked up, they saw four horse legs protruding through the ceiling above them.

Chocolate Fudge Cake

This recipe belonged to Mary Stewart, wife of a former member of the North-West Mounted Police. After her husband's retirement from the force they moved to Leavings, now Granum, Alberta. There she operated a boarding house, which became renowned for its excellent food.[6]

1/2 cup [125 mL] butter
1-1/2 cups [375 mL] sugar
2 eggs, beaten
1 tsp [5 mL] vanilla
1-3/4 cups [450 mL] all-purpose flour
1/3 cup [75 mL] cocoa
1 tsp [5 mL] cream of tartar
1/2 tsp [2 mL] salt
1/2 cup [125 mL] milk
1 tsp [5 mL] baking soda
3/4 cup [175 mL] boiling water

Cream butter and sugar together; add eggs and vanilla. Beat well. Sift flour, cocoa, cream of tartar and salt. Stir into batter alternately with milk. Dissolve soda in boiling water and beat into the batter until smooth. Pour into two 8 or 9 inch [20 to 23 cm] well-buttered and floured layer cake tins. Bake at 300° F [150° C] for 35 to 40 minutes. Cool 10 minutes, loosen and turn upside down on a wire rack. When cool, frost the layers with Chocolate Butter Icing or Caramel Icing.

Note: This cake can also be baked in a 9x13 inch [23x33 cm] rectangular pan. It will require approximately 45 to 50 minutes.

Regal Chocolate Sauce

This is an old recipe from Mary Stewart's handwritten cookbook. It makes a delicious sauce for ice cream, puddings and cake.

Makes approximately 3/4 cup [175 mL] sauce
2 squares unsweetened chocolate
1/2 cup [125 mL] water
1/2 cup [125 mL] sugar
1-1/2 tbsp [25 mL] butter
pinch salt
2 tsp [10 mL] vanilla

Heat chocolate, water and sugar in a heavy saucepan or a double boiler over low heat until the chocolate is melted. Add butter, salt and vanilla; mix well and simmer for 5 minutes. Beat until smooth. If you prefer a thinner sauce, add water until it reaches the desired consistency.

LAST RANGE ON THE RANCH

"Think of the delight of this clear air, and let the housekeeper in you think of the appetite which this air gives men and women (though we do not count much in this way here), and the huge meals that must be forthcoming at regular times every day. We have a cow camp and a shack for the cowboys—and they have their own cook so we only get an occasional one for meals if he happens to be riding nearer the house than the camp. They are a nice lot of men. I love their attempt to help me to appear civilized. Though they ride in flannel shirts, they never come to the table in shirt sleeves. There is a black alpaca coat, which hangs in the shack attached to the house, for the cowboys' use, and each one struggles into it to live up to the new regime which began with a bride at the ranche and this is done with such good will that I have no qualms of conscience that I am a nuisance.

The cowboys back me in all attempts and indeed in all my schemes because I ride well. I verily believe if I did not ride they would have nothing to do with me, as it is, they are rather proud of me....

I am twenty miles from a woman and though I like all the men and enjoy having them visit I simply long to talk to a woman. About once a month I ride into Saint Francis with Geof and stay a night with my dearest friend Mrs. Milner.... It does me good to talk

Mrs. Sarah Gardiner on Fly. She was an excellent rider and continued to ride sidesaddle long after it was permissible for women to ride regular saddles.
Photo credit: Museum of the Highwood

to her, and every man loves her, not in a sighing silly way, but because she always makes them comfortable, darns their clothes and talks to them sternly if they are doing anything wrong. I am sure that she has done more good than two parsons.

I love the freedom of my life and try to make everyone about me share a bit in my happiness. My life may seem rough and bare, but there is something to compensate one for every hardship and trial. You must come to see me though, for it is the spirit of the west that charms one, and I cannot convey it to you, try as I may. It is a shy, wild spirit and will not leave its native mountains and rolling prairies and though I try to get it into my letters I fail, but I must warn you that if it once charms you it becomes an obsession, and one grows very lonely away from it. No Westerner who has ever felt its fascination ever is really content in the conventional East.

P.S. Do tell me what the newest hats are like."
from the letters of Mary Inderwick[7]

Strawberry Shortcake

Historically, strawberry shortcake was served when the wild strawberries ripened in the meadows. The shortcake was a rich biscuit dough baked in a round cake pan. The following recipe was taken from Mrs. George Treadway's handwritten recipe book, dated 1898 and now part of the historic collection in the museum at High River, Alberta.

Serves 6

2 cups [500 m] flour

4 tsp [20 mL] baking powder

1/4 tsp [1 mL] cream of tartar

1/4 tsp [1 mL] salt

1/2 cup [125 mL] fat [butter or shortening]

2/3 cup [150 mL] milk

4 cups [1 L] strawberries

1/4 cup [50 mL] sugar

Sift flour, baking powder, cream of tartar and salt together. Work in fat with your fingers until mixture resembles coarse crumbs. Stir in milk gradually. Place dough on a lightly floured board. Divide into 2 parts and roll each part to fit a round cake pan. Place first layer into lightly greased cake tin. Brush the dough with melted butter, then place second layer over top.

Bake at 400° F [200° C] for 20 minutes. Reserve approximately 12 choice berries for the top. Mash the remaining berries slightly, stir in sugar and place sweetened berries between the layers. Cover the top layer with Sweetened Flavoured Whipped Cream and garnish with whole berries.

Note: The biscuit dough may be rolled and cut into round shapes as for tea biscuits, then split into halves for strawberry or peach shortcake.

Sweetened Flavoured Whipped Cream

1/2 pint [250 mL] whipping cream

2 tbsp [30 mL] sugar

1 tsp [5 mL] vanilla

Beat the cream until thick. Fold in sugar and vanilla.

Mabel Biggs turning her barrel churn by a crank located
on the side. After the butter formed, she would pour in cold
water from the nearby well to wash it. c. 1908.
Photo credit: Glenbow Archives

Prune Pie

Many women were totally unprepared for their new life in the Canadian West. The men on one ranch had longed for a woman's touch around the place and looked forward to a new bride's arrival with great anticipation. Her suitcase was hardly unpacked when they urged her to make a prune pie. Although she had never baked a pie in her life, she gamely proceeded to work out a method to fit their description of what a prune pie should be. She prepared a bottom crust, heaped in the dried prunes [with no presoaking or simmering], covered it all with a top crust and baked it for a good long time.

The men on that ranch exemplified the ultimate gallantry, for they never uttered a word of complaint as they hacked and cut their way through that pie.

Pie Pastry

During the eighteen years that Sally Smith cooked at the A7 Ranch in Alberta, she baked four pies almost every day [besides bread, cake and muffins]. Each ranch hand had his turn choosing the kind of pie to be made the next day.

Flaky pastry for pies and meat toppings was made with home-rendered lard. Any ranch wife worth her salt could "make up" and "roll out" half a dozen pies while her bread was in the oven.

Makes 2 single-crust pies or 1 double-crust pie

2 cups [500 mL] all-purpose flour
1 tsp [5 mL] salt
3/4 cup [175 mL] lard, cold
5 to 7 tbsp [75 to 100 mL] cold water

Sift flour and salt together. With fingers, work lard into flour until mixture looks like coarse meal. Sprinkle water on top. Gather dough together with your hands and work into a ball. Roll out less than 1/8 inch [1/3 cm] thick, on a floured board.

Saskatoon Pie

Berry picking was generally regarded as a task for women and children. During berry season a rancher's wife tied empty lard pails to the saddle and rode to a stream bank or a dry slope where the saskatoon berries grew. When she returned home, she soaked the berries for an hour or so in lightly salted water to draw out the occasional worm that might otherwise have gone unnoticed.

4 cups [1 L] saskatoons
1/4 cup [50 mL] water
2 tbsp [30 mL] lemon juice or vinegar
3/4 cup [175 mL] sugar
3 tbsp [45 mL] flour
1/4 tsp [1 mL] salt
1/4 tsp [1mL] almond flavouring

Place saskatoons and water in a heavy saucepan. Cover and bring to a boil. Turn off the heat and steam for 5 minutes. Add lemon juice and flavouring. Mix sugar, flour and salt; blend with the saskatoons and liquid. Pour into an unbaked pastry shell. Cover with a pastry top. Make 2 or 3 small slits for steam to escape. Bake in a 400° F [200° C] oven for 35 to 40 minutes or until lightly browned.

Sit up for a Meal

When Bea Godden returned from England, she was met in Calgary by her fiance Henry Sheppard. They were married that day and started at once for their home on the Paleface Ranch, some distance away.

They travelled as far as Pine Creek Stopping Place the first night and arrived at the High River Horse Ranch about supper time the next day. Manager Phil Weinard invited them to have supper and stay the night.

In their honour, he set the table with a fine white tablecloth, silverware and beautiful cut glass—all brought from England by the previous owner. By this time the new bride was quite impressed with ranch life and sat at the table with expectations of a splendid supper. At last the first and only course was brought in—a big, black, iron pot full of cornmeal mush.[8]

It was the custom of the country to invite guests "to sit up for a meal" with no embarrassment or apology if there was a meagre supply of food on hand.

Ranch house west of Fort Macleod, Alberta. c. 1888.
Photo credit: Glenbow Archives

Beefsteak and Kidney Pie

Serves 8 to 10

4 pounds [2kg] blade or chuck steak cut into 1 inch [2.5 cm] pieces

1/2 to 3/4 pound [250-375 g] lamb or beef kidney

4 tbsp [60 mL] beef fat or lard

2 medium onions, minced

2/3 cup [150 mL] flour

2 tsp [10 mL] salt

1/2 tsp [2 mL] freshly ground pepper

4 cups [1 L] beef broth [canned or water and beef bouillon cubes]

2 tsp [10 mL] prepared mustard

1-1/2 tbsp [20 mL] Worcestershire sauce

1/2 tsp [2 mL] cinnamon

1 tsp [5 mL] ginger

2 cups [500 mL] mushrooms, sliced [optional]

pie pastry for topping

Melt fat in a Dutch oven; brown beef and kidney. Add onion and sauté. Mix flour, salt and pepper. Sprinkle over meat and stir. Add beef broth, mustard, Worcestershire sauce, cinnamon and ginger. Cover and simmer over low heat until tender, about 2-1/2 hours, or bake in a 300° F [150° C] oven until tender. Add mushrooms. If the liquid is too thin, thicken with flour mixed to a paste with water. If too thick, thin with red wine or water.

Grease a 9x13 inch [23x33 cm] baking dish. Add the meat and liquid. Cool. In the meantime prepare the pie pastry. Place over meat, moistening and pinching to the edge of the dish. Make vents in the pastry to allow steam to escape. Bake in hot oven 450° F [230° C] for 10 minutes, lower heat to moderate 375° F [190° C] and continue baking for 15 minutes or until the pie crust is golden brown.

Corn Bread

Corn Bread or Johnny Cake was baked in cake tins, cast iron frying pans or muffin tins. It was served hot with butter and jam for breakfast, as an accompaniment to a main course or with syrup for dessert.

1-1/2 cups [375 mL] cornmeal

2-1/2 cups [625 mL] milk

2 eggs, beaten

1/2 cup [125 mL] melted fat or cooking oil

2 cups [500 mL] flour

3/4 cup [175 mL] sugar

2 tbsp [30 mL] baking powder

1 tsp [5 mL] salt

Combine cornmeal, milk, eggs and fat. Let stand for 10 minutes. Sift flour, sugar, baking powder and salt together. Stir into cornmeal mixture. Grease a 9x13 inch [23x33 cm] cake can or a large cast iron frying pan. Pour in batter. Bake at 400° F [200° C] for approximately 30 minutes. Alternately, bake in greased muffin pans for about 15 to 20 minutes.

LIFE ON A RANCH, 1898

"It is true that we do not scatter visiting cards or make many afternoon calls, for reasons connected with time and space and other large considerations. We do not give each other dinner parties but we give each other dinner, generally at 1 p.m., and beds for the night. People usually come when they have some reason for passing this way; and in ranching country, houses are so few and far between that hospitality of necessity becomes a matter of course. People do not expect to be entertained. We have no means of formally entertaining each other, and it is not thought amusing to talk from morning to night. A visitor prefers to smoke his pipe in peace, to find his way out and wander around the corrals to inspect any bit of building going on, or to cast a critical eye on the stock. After which he saddles his "cayuse" and departs on his own affairs.

A small rider in a specially constructed basket saddle in front of the Bedingfeld Ranch House. A few years later, this ranch was purchased by Edward, Prince of Wales, and became known throughout the world as the E.P. Ranch. c. 1913. Photo credit: Glenbow Archives

I like the simplicity, the informality of life, the long hours in the open air. I like riding over the endless prairie, the wind sweeping the grass, the great silent sunshine, the vast skies and the splendid line of the Rockies guarding the West. I like herds of cattle feeding among the foothills, moving slowly from water to water. I like the clear rivers that come pouring out of the mountains, and the little lakes among the hills where the wild ducks drop down to rest on their flight to the north. I like the work and play. I like the summer and winter, the monotony and the changes. Besides I like a flannel shirt and liberty."[9]

Mrs. Walter Skrine, using the pen name Moira O'Neill, describes her life in the Alberta foothills west of High River.

Prince of Wales Cake

Edward, Prince of Wales, visited Alberta and purchased the E.P. Ranch in the early 1900s. He must have expressed a liking for spice cakes because recipes for Prince of Wales Cake appeared in High River cookbooks about that time. This is a traditional Raisin Spice Cake that is moist and delicious.

2 cups [500 mL] raisins

2-1/2 cups [625 mL] water

2 cups [500 mL] brown sugar

1 cup [250 mL] butter or oil

2 eggs

1 tsp [5 mL] vanilla

2-3/4 cups [675 mL] flour

1 tsp [5 mL] salt

2 tsp [10 mL] baking powder

1 tsp [5 mL] baking soda

2 tsp [10 mL] cinnamon

1 tsp [5 mL] nutmeg

Combine raisins and water in a saucepan, simmer 5 minutes. Cool. Cream butter, sugar, eggs and vanilla. Add cooled raisin water. In a large bowl sift together dry ingredients and gradually stir creamed mixture into the dry ingredients. Fold in raisins.

Pour batter into a 9x13 inch [23x33 cm] greased cake pan. Bake in a 350° F [180° C] oven for 40 minutes or until cake tester comes out clean.

Caramel Icing

The flavour of this easy-to-prepare icing tastes very good on chocolate cake and Prince of Wales cake.

Makes sufficient for a 9x13 inch [23x33 cm] cake

1/4 cup [50 mL] butter

1 cup [250 mL] brown sugar

1/4 cup [50 mL] milk

1 tsp [5 mL] vanilla

1 to 1-1/2 cups [250-375 mL] icing sugar

Melt the butter in a heavy saucepan. Add brown sugar and stir over heat for 2 minutes. Add milk and bring to boil. Remove from heat; add vanilla. Cool slightly. Beat in enough icing sugar to make a spreading consistency. Spread on cooled cake.

THE FIRST BREAD

Erica Woodward recalled: "We had just moved to our place near Swift Current and mother had never tried making bread before. There she was in the kitchen, banging the cupboard doors, slamming the oven of the new Kitchen Queen, tears of frustration in her eyes, angry words on her lips. Dad heard the commotion and came in. He took one look at those hard, brown blocks spread out on the kitchen table and then went over and put his arms around her.

Next morning he woke us children and motioned us to follow him to the creek bank where he had only yesterday cut steps in the moist clay. He stopped at the first step, fished one of the dry loaves out of his bag, set it firmly on the clay step, marked its size, lifted it, cut a neat hole, then fitted the loaf perfectly into the hole to form a step. Then he embedded the second loaf in the second step and the third loaf in the third step and right down the line until the six loaves graced the six steps as if they had been made for that purpose. Then we fetched mother to share in the admiration of our new concrete-like steps leading to the creek. Well, we all laughed so hard we hardly had strength to make it back to the house.

But mother was not beaten. She tackled bread baking again and again and soon was able to turn out six beautiful, golden crusted loaves. Dad while munching a sample with obvious satisfaction said it was just as well since there were no more steps to make."[10]

Mrs. Fred Ings feeding poultry at the Midway Ranch, Nanton, Alberta, c. 1911.
Photo credit: Glenbow Archives

Air Buns

Bread making used to require the preparation of a flour yeast sponge the night before baking. If kept warm all night, this sponge would be nicely risen by morning, no small task in houses with wood-burning stoves and fires that died out. Ranch wife Monica Hopkins wrote: "These evenings I wrap my bread in a blanket and Billie's fur coat, put it in one of the wicker chairs and cover all up with a travelling rug and you should see it next morning, right up to the very top of the bread pan."[11] Fast-rising yeasts available today enable completion of bread making within three hours of starting. This recipe produces feather-light buns that can be served anytime, picnics, brandings and barbecues.

Makes 48 buns

1/2 cup [125 mL] warm water
1 tsp [5 mL] sugar
1 tbsp [15 mL] yeast [1 package]
3-1/2 cups [875 mL] warm water
1/2 cup [125 mL] sugar
1/2 cup [125 mL] vegetable oil
2 tsp [10 mL] salt
1 tbsp [15 mL] vanilla
8 to 10 cups [2 to 2.5 L] flour

Pour the 1/2 cup [125 mL] of water into a large mixing bowl. Dissolve sugar, sprinkle yeast on top and leave for 10 minutes. Combine remaining water and sugar and vegetable oil, salt, and vanilla and add to the yeast mixture. Beat in as much of the flour as possible; knead in the remainder. Knead well for 8 to 10 minutes. Cover with a tea towel and leave in a warm place to rise for 1 hour. Shape the dough into round buns and place on a cookie sheet, about 20 to a 12x18 inch [30x45 cm] sheet. Cover with a tea towel and let rise for approximately 1-1/2 hours. Bake at 400° F [200° C] for 12 to 15 minutes.

Cinnamon Rolls

Use about 1/2 of the Air Bun dough for this recipe. It will also require butter or margarine, brown sugar, white sugar and cinnamon.

Prepare the pan: Melt 1/4 cup [50 mL] of butter or margarine in a large cake pan, 9x13 inches [23x33 cm]. Cover with a sprinkling of brown sugar, enough to make a thin layer of the butter-sugar mixture. Sprinkle with 2 teaspoons [10 mL] of cinnamon and 1 tablespoon [15 mL] of water.

Prepare the rolls: Roll the bread dough into an oblong of 9x18 inches [23x46 cm]. Spread with 3 tablespoons [45 mL] of softened butter or margarine. Sprinkle with 1/2 cup [125 mL] of white sugar and 4 teaspoons [20 mL] of cinnamon.

Beginning at the wide side, roll up and pinch the edges together. Cut the roll into 1 inch [2.5 cm] slices and place the slices a little apart in the prepared cake pan. Cover with a tea towel and let rise until double in bulk, 35 to 40 minutes. Bake at 375° F [190° C] for 25 to 30 minutes. [A Pyrex pan takes a little less time.] Remove the rolls from the oven immediately and invert the pan.

A BAKE OVEN

As a bride, Susan Louisa Allison rode sidesaddle over the rugged Hope Trail to become the first white woman to settle in the Similkameen Valley. Shortly after, she and her husband established a ranch called Sunnyside [now Westbank] on the Okanagan Lake. She became a good neighbour to the surrounding Indians and from them learned to cure fish and dry venison. After she had lost two homes, one to fire and one to flood, the family lived for a time in a tent. With her children's help, she built an outdoor bake oven and continued to produce delicious meals.

"It was hard work cooking without a stove. I thought that with all hands helping I could build a bake oven. This I did on the banks of a river using cobblestones and clay. All hands gathered the stones, Will and Beatrice mixed mud, Lily packed it to me and I built it. Someone found a half melted door from the old stove which made a good door for the new oven.

Susan Allison was the first white woman to settle in Similkameen; her eldest son Edgar was born there. Later they built a ranch near Lake Okanagan called Sunnyside [now known as Westbank]. Photo credit: Provincial Archives of British Columbia

One day near June I had put three ducks nicely dressed, and a huge custard into the oven, and all was cooked ready to be eaten by hungry people. I had no tea or coffee so I browned some dried peas and used them for coffee, which was also ready. Two well-dressed men rode up and said they were starving so I gave them something to eat…. I dished up the dinner and told them to sit down. I thought there would be enough for us but no, they ate all the ducks and pudding. They talked French thinking I couldn't understand them. They said my bread was like cake and the ducks the best they had ever tasted. I felt proud of the oven after that."[12]

Roast Wild Duck

Hunting was and is still both a sport and a means of providing fresh meat for the table.

Serves 4

2 average-sized ducks

1/4 cup [50 mL] oil

1 tsp [5 mL] salt

1/4 tsp [1 mL] pepper

6 strips bacon

1 can consommé or 1 cup [250 mL] beef broth

1/4 cup [50 mL] Madeira wine

The ducks should be plucked, drawn and washed. Remove any pinfeathers. Mix the oil, salt, and pepper and brush over skin surface. Place birds on a rack in a roasting pan, breast side up. Cover with bacon strips.

Roast at 425° F [220° C] for approximately 1 to 1-1/2 hours [depending on whether you like duck rare, medium or well done].

Remove from oven. Skim off most of fat in pan. Stir consommé and Madeira wine into the drippings. Heat. Serve ducks on a platter with Madeira sauce in a gravy bowl. Drizzle the sauce over the ducks.

Rhubarb Crisp

This dessert is served in early summer.

Serves 5 to 6

4 cups [1 L] rhubarb, cut into small pieces

1/2 cup [125 mL] sugar

1 tbsp [15 mL] flour

1/4 tsp [1 mL] cinnamon

Place rhubarb pieces in a 9 inch [23 cm] square or equivalent sized casserole. Combine sugar, flour and cinnamon. Mix with rhubarb.

Crumbly Crust Top

3/4 cup [175 mL] brown sugar, firmly packed

1/3 cup [75 mL] butter or margarine

1 cup [250 mL] flour

1 tsp [5 mL] cinnamon

Mix the ingredients until butter resembles coarse crumbs. Sprinkle over rhubarb. Bake at 375° F [190° C] for 30 to 40 minutes or until rhubarb is tender.

THE RANCH HOME

"There was work for every season. Summer was spent breaking horses, rounding up cattle, branding, calving, seeding, haying, fencing, butchering. During winter special care was given to the livestock, supplying feed, keeping a water hole open, fending off coyotes and wolves, and mending harnesses. It was quite a job to organize and keep a ranch household running smoothly. Everyone helped. When children weren't studying, they worked on the ranch: chopping wood, haying, fencing, cooking, washing dishes, cleaning house and churning butter.

The ranch house was home, school and social centre to fifteen people, counting nine members of the family, the hired help, and a school governess who lived and held school in the big room upstairs.

There were always extra people dropping in for a meal. Planks were added to the end of the dining room table until it became so long it extended right into the kitchen. Meals were informal, the food hearty and healthy. Nothing was wasted. A bone was turned into soup, with even the beef marrow eaten. Extra milk made cheese; doughnuts were made with extra lard; dried bread was the basis for bread pudding.

We drove to town two or three times a year and loaded up on supplies: one hundred pounds of honey; cases of dried fruit; five barrels of apples every fall; one-hundred-pound bags of sugar and flour, each in five-bag lots.

Most of the food came from the ranch itself. A cow and a pig were butchered and the meat put up for later use as corned beef, canned beef, hams, bacon, sausages. Chickens were raised for eggs and Sunday dinner. The vegetable garden provided fresh greens all summer and enough potatoes, turnips and carrots to store in the root house for winter use.

Wild berries, saskatoons, chokecherries and goose-berries were made into jam and preserves. Milk was separated, the cream used for butter and baking, the milk for drinking and puddings.

There was fun as well as work. We had taffy pulls and hymn singing on Sunday nights. There were summer picnics and parties to which everyone went—children, parents and the hired help."[13]

Annie McKinnon Fuller, daughter of Sarah and Lachlan McKinnon, recalling her childhood on the L K Ranch.

Opposite: The Lachlan McKinnon children on the L K Ranch, Dalemead. Building the L K into a beautiful and prosperous Alberta ranch was a family enterprise. c. 1910. Photo credit: Glenbow Archives

Ranch House Meat Loaf

The aroma of Meat Loaf wafting from a ranch kitchen on a winter day is ambrosia to a hungry cowhand.

Serves 6

2 pounds [1 kg] ground beef

1/2 cup [125 mL] onion, finely chopped

1 cup [250 mL] bread or cracker crumbs

2 eggs

3/4 of 10 oz [284 mL] can beef broth

1 tsp [5 mL] salt

1 tsp [5 mL] parsley

1 tsp [5 mL] sage

1 tsp [5mL] thyme

1/4 tsp [1 mL] pepper

Mix all the meat loaf ingredients together. Pack into a 5x9 inch [13x23 cm] loaf pan. Bake at 325° F [160° C] for 1-1/4 hours. Remove from oven, turn out of pan and place on an ovenproof serving dish.

Topping

3 tbsp [45 mL] brown sugar

4 tbsp [60 mL] ketchup

1 tsp [5 mL] dry mustard

Mix the topping ingredients. Brush over the meat loaf and return to the oven for 30 minutes [or longer].

Luella Goddard on the Bow River Horse Ranch near Cochrane, Alberta. Women usually made their own clothes and were skilled in the art of needlework. c. early 1900s.
Photo credit: Glenbow Archives

SHE'S UP TO CHEESE

Sickness was a problem on a lonely ranch. An assortment of home remedies was always kept on hand, hoping that one would cure the patient and thus spare the long, hard ride to find a doctor. A rancher's wife recalled one of her home nursing experiences:

"One day a frantic neighbour came to fetch me. A lady visitor at his ranch was in great pain, with suspected pleurisy. I was the nearest woman. Would I help? Of course, I rode over and undertook the task of nursing the patient back to health. The neighbour's son helped assemble the ingredients for a mustard plaster and a clean flour sack to put it in. The patient fought like a tiger but we finally got it on her. Next, I asked for a thermometer. The neighbour's son said they had one and produced a dairy thermometer a foot long and half an inch thick, made of clear glass. We were afraid to put it into her mouth for fear she would bite it off. After some thought it was decided to put it under her arm. I leaned over and held her arm down tight while the young man watched the glass. A full minute passed, then I asked, "What is her temperature?" He replied, "She's up to cheese."

In spite of us she recovered and was able to go home the next day. It was just a touch of acute indigestion."[14]

Scalloped Corn Casserole

This winter vegetable dish can be served with beef, ham, pork chops, sausages or meat loaf.

Serves 6
2 14-oz [398 mL] cans creamed corn
2 beaten eggs
3/4 cup [175 mL] milk
1 tsp [5 mL] salt
1/4 tsp [1 mL] freshly ground black pepper
3/4 cup [175 mL] soda cracker crumbs
3 tbsp [45 mL] butter, melted

Mix corn, eggs, milk, salt and pepper in a casserole. Mix half the crackers with the corn mixture. Mix the other half with the butter and sprinkle on top of corn mixture. Bake in a 325° F [160° C] oven for about 1 hour.

Pickled Beets

This was a popular pickle, probably because beets are easy to grow. Small young beets are best, but large beets can be used successfully, too.

Makes approximately 8 pint [or 0.5 L] jars
6 pounds [3 kg] beets
4 cups [1 L] vinegar
2 cups [500 mL] water
3 cups [750 mL] sugar
1 tbsp [15 mL] mixed pickling spices

Cook beets in boiling water until tender [up to 2 hours]. Peel. If beets are large, cut them into thick slices; if small, leave whole. Combine vinegar, sugar and spices. Bring to a boil and simmer for 10 minutes. Pack beets into sterilized jars and cover with hot liquid. Seal and store in a cool place.

THE SCHOOLHOUSE

The local school was the centre of social life and the locale of box socials, pie socials, picnics and the annual Christmas concert.

Box socials were community dances for which each lady prepared a splendid lunch and packed it into a fancy box. The men bid on the boxes auction style, with the highest bidder winning the box and the right to eat supper with the owner of the box. Inside the box were slices of chicken, cold ham or corned beef; fresh home-made buns, sandwiches of potted meat, canned salmon or egg salad; pickles; generous slices of sponge cake, fruit cake and mincemeat tarts. White china cups were passed out and someone carried large enamel pots around the room and filled each cup with coffee or tea.

Pies were a favourite food among bachelor cowboys, so for variety the box socials were sometimes replaced by pie socials. Ladies made their specialty—saskatoon, rhubarb, raisin, apple or custard—and the whole pie was auctioned off to the highest bidder. One pie-hungry cowboy bought three pies, then sat right down and ate them without a pause.

Everyone went to the Christmas concerts. There was an organized program of recitations, plays and songs, with every child participating. After that Santa Claus bounded in the schoolhouse door and from his gunnysack pack brought out a small gift for each child. Then he passed out candies and oranges to everyone. When the concert was over, the men piled the desks into a corner of the schoolhouse and the fiddler drew out his fiddle for an hour or two of dancing before it was time to go home.

Sugar Cookies

This recipe yields cookies similar to the memorable crisp ones that Charlie Yuen baked for the Bow River ranch foreman's little daughter.

1 cup [250 mL] butter

1-1/4 cups [300 mL] sugar

1 egg

1 tsp [5 mL] vanilla

1 tsp [5 mL] baking soda

1 tsp [5 mL] cream of tartar

1/2 tsp [2 mL] salt

2-1/2 cups [625 mL] flour

Cream butter and sugar. Beat in egg and vanilla. Sift soda, cream of tartar, salt and flour together, then add to creamed mixture. Refrigerate for 2 or 3 hours [or overnight]. Roll out on a well-floured board and cut with a round cookie cutter. Bake on a cookie sheet at 375° F [190° C] for approximately 8 minutes [until lightly browned].

Ginger Snaps

This recipe makes good old-fashioned ginger snaps with a crinkly top. The dough can also be rolled out thin and cut with a cookie cutter for thin crisp cookies.

3/4 cup [175 mL] margarine

1 cup [250 mL] sugar

1 egg

1/4 cup [50 mL] molasses

2 cups [500 mL] flour

1 tsp [5 mL] baking soda

1/2 tsp [2 mL] salt

1 tbsp [15 mL] ginger

1 tsp [5 mL] cinnamon

1/4 tsp [1 mL] cloves

Cream margarine and sugar; beat in egg and molasses. Sift dry ingredients together and add to the creamed mixture. Roll the dough into small balls [1 tsp size] and place on greased cookie sheet. Bake at 350° F [180° C]. If you like a slightly soft centre bake for 15 to 20 minutes. For a crisper cookie bake at least 20 minutes.

Christmas Gingerbread Cookies: Roll dough out on a lightly floured board, cut with cookie cutter, bake approximately 12 minutes. Frost with butter icing and decorate.

Opposite: Little Katie riding a pig. Animals were very important in the lives of ranch children, who cared for and frequently made pets of them. Photo credit: Glenbow Archives

DANCING

Before the turn of the century, the North-West Mounted Police posts were the centre of social life, and their dances were great events on the social calendar. Thirteen police balls were held in 1880 at Fort Walsh. The three white women living there at the time—Mrs. Macleod, Mrs. Winder and Mrs. Shurtliff—attended, as well as many of the local half-breed ladies.

Mothers always took their babies to the dances and left them on a nearby bed where they slept undisturbed. The exception was one occasion at which a couple of the cowboys thought that it would be great fun to switch baby clothes, bonnets and blankets. When the dancing was over, the mothers sleepily picked up their babies and went home. The next morning when they saw a strange baby there was great consternation and a long ride around the country to find the right baby.[15]

After the country became settled, people took turns having dances in their homes. It was a way of meeting neighbours and preventing loneliness. When the weather was cold and the snow deep, they hitched a team of good horses to a sleigh box. Rocks were heated and buried in straw to keep their feet warm and buffalo robes were pulled over their laps. During the summer months they rode saddle horses. One thought nothing of riding a horse twelve miles to a dance, with a good suit of clothes or a dress packed in a gunnysack tied to the saddle.

The fiddle, mouth organ and accordion ground out such favourite tunes as "The Heel Toe Polka," "The Log Cabin Jersey," Rye Waltz," "Marching through Georgia" and "Highland Schottische."

Opposite: A home orchestra near Maple Creek, Saskatchewan, in 1913. Ranching families made their own fun. The walls made from squared logs have been given a light coat of calcimine. On the right is a picture of Queen Victoria.
Photo credit: Glenbow Archives

There were no wallflowers in a country with three men to every woman. The men were so anxious to dance that they sometimes tied a handkerchief around one arm signifying a willingness to be regarded as a lady partner.

Dances lasted all night, partly because the people were young and vibrant, partly because it was safer to wait until dawn to find one's way home across the dark countryside.

Jelly Roll

Katie Moffatt brought a jelly roll to a North-West Mounted Police Dance at the Regina barracks in 1890.[16] Note: This cake may be baked in two 8 inch [20 cm] round tins and filled as a layer cake.

3 eggs, separated
3/4 cup [175 mL] sugar
1 tsp [5 mL] vanilla
2 tbsp [30 mL] butter
1/2 cup [125 mL] water
1 cup [250 mL] flour
1 tsp [5 mL] baking powder
1/4 tsp [1 mL] salt

Preheat oven to 400° F [200° C]. Line a 15x10 inch [39x26 cm] jelly roll pan with wax paper, grease it well and sprinkle lightly with flour. Beat egg whites until fluffy. Add sugar gradually and beat until sugar has dissolved and whites stand in peaks. Add egg yolks and beat until thick and creamy. Add vanilla.

Heat butter and water [do not boil]. Sift flour, baking powder and salt. Add at one time to the egg-sugar mixture, then fold in lightly. Add all the hot liquid at one time and fold gently. Spread out in a jelly roll pan. Bake approximately 12 minutes.

While it is hot, invert cake onto a tea towel sprinkled with confectioner's sugar. Cut off hard edges. Spread cake with raspberry jam or Lemon Butter; roll it. Wrap in saran wrap or wax paper to keep.

Lemon Butter Filling

Lemons were scarce and were treats saved for special occasions.

2 large lemons [or juice to measure, approximately 6 tbsp/100 mL]
1 tsp [5 mL] grated lemon rind
1/4 cup [50 mL] butter
2 large eggs, beaten
1 cup [250 mL] sugar

Wash and dry a 16 ounce [500 mL] glass jar; keep it warm. Wash and dry lemons; grate rind very finely. Squeeze juice from the lemons. Place lemon rind, juice, butter, eggs and sugar in a mixing bowl or top of a double boiler. Set saucepan with a small amount of water and simmer on low heat. Stir mixture for 15 to 20 minutes, until it thickens, but do not allow it to boil. Pour into the heated jar. Lemon Butter will keep in refrigerator for up to 6 weeks if tightly covered. Serve in baked tart shells, or as a filling for Jelly Roll or Yard Cake [Cowboys and Chuckwagons].

Gingerbread

Gingerbread can be served as a cake. It is particularly good served warm with sweetened, flavoured whipped cream. For an elegant dessert, decorate with slivers of candied ginger.

2-1/2 cups [625 mL] flour
2 tsp [10 mL] ginger
1 tsp [5 mL] cinnamon
1/4 tsp [1 mL] cloves
1/4 tsp [1 mL] salt
1 tsp [5 mL] baking soda
1 cup [250 mL] brown sugar
1/2 cup [125 mL] melted butter or margarine
1 cup [250 mL] fancy molasses
2 eggs
1 cup [250 mL] boiling water

Preheat oven to 350° F [180° C]. Sift flour, spices, salt and soda together. In a large bowl stir sugar into melted butter or margarine. Add molasses and eggs and beat well. Add dry ingredients alternately with water, beating thoroughly after each addition. Pour into a greased 9x13 inch [23x33 cm] pan and bake at 350° F [180° C] for 40 to 50 minutes.

Dances of Soda Creek

Early ranchers in the isolated Cariboo country of British Columbia took every opportunity to have some fun. One lonely wife recalled: "One day during winter my husband heard there was to be a dance at Soda Creek. We loved to dance and decided to go. Times were hard. It cost 50 cents to go to a dance so this was a big event for us.

As we came into town we saw a big barrel with a dipper attached to its rim by an "S" wire standing right in the middle of the road in front of the hotel. The dipper must have held a pint at least.

My curious husband went to look. He filled the dipper and tasted the contents. Then I took a drink and it was the nicest tasting stuff. It was rhubarb wine. We found out that old Charlie Ross [a neighbour] placed a barrel there every time there was a dance and it was free to everyone."[17]

Rhubarb Juice

Rhubarb, called the spring tonic, makes a refreshing, attractive summer drink and is a good base for a party punch.

8 pounds [4 kg] rhubarb	
3 quarts [3 L] water	
3 cups [750 mL] sugar	

Wash and cut rhubarb into small pieces. Add water and simmer slowly until the rhubarb is very soft. Strain to make 1 gallon [4 L] of juice. Cook juice and sugar until boiling. Store in the refrigerator. Serve juice cold. It can also be mixed with equal proportions of 7-Up, ginger ale or carbonated lemon-lime drink.

Lemonade

This lemonade concentrate is easy to pack for a community picnic and handy to keep in the refrigerator at home.

8 lemons	
4 tbsp [60 mL] citric acid	
2 tbsp [30 mL] tartaric acid	
1 tbsp [15 mL] epsom salts	
8 cups [2 L] sugar	
rind of 4 lemons	
6 cups [1.5 L] boiling water	

Squeeze juice from lemons. Mix all ingredients and leave for 24 hours, then strain and store in a covered jar. To mix, use 2 tablespoons [30 mL] per glass of cold water, or 1/2 cup [125 mL] per quart [1 L] of cold water, or 2 cups [500 mL] per 4 quarts [4 L] of cold water.

THE HISTORIC O'KEEFE RANCH

Sleigh bells jingled on Christmas Day as people from Vernon and the surrounding countryside arrived at the ranch in horse drawn cutters to attend the Open House.

Mary Ann O'Keefe.
Photo credit: The Historic O'Keefe Ranch

Cornelius and Mary Ann O'Keefe loved to entertain graciously and lavishly every Christmas Day in their elegant home near Vernon in the North Okanagan Valley. Champagne toasts started off the merriment. Then guests visited and helped themselves to the table laden with specialities such as Cold Tongue in Mold, Spiced Beef, Jellied Aspics, Fruit Cake, Ginger Cakes, Shortbread and Ginger Cookies for the children. These had all been prepared by the family cook Louis Wong under the watchful eye of Mrs. O'Keefe.

The ranch remained a centre of social activity and remained in the family for ninety-one years before becoming an historic site.

The family had much to be thankful for. Life had not always been easy. Mary Ann came as a bride to a log house heated only by two stoves, one in the kitchen and one in the parlour. Cooking, baking, eating, bathing, laundry and dressing were all done in the kitchen. There was no indoor plumbing. Roads were primitive and the ranch at first was isolated. She was one of only a few white women in the whole Okanagan Valley.

Here Mary Ann bore nine children in ten years, so when her husband was able to build the lovely Queen Ann-style mansion there was cause for celebration.

Mary Ann enjoyed her new home for only thirteen years before she died of a massive stroke. Later Cornelius married Elizabeth Tierney, forty years younger than himself, and they had five more children.[18]

Tongue in Mold

At the turn of the century, fashionable hostesses served jellied tongue at picnics, card parties, dances and receptions. This recipe was developed by Bessie Emms, who was born near Wainwright but spent most of her life in Calgary. She suggested unmolding it for the buffet table, slicing thinly and serving on a dark bread with a dab of mustard sauce.

Fresh tongue should be soaked in the corned beef brine for 3 weeks before cooking, or if you prefer, purchase a pickled tongue from your butcher. [Large tongues are somewhat coarser in texture than small tongues.]

Cooking the Tongue

1 pickled tongue

2 cups [500 mL] fruit juice [apple, orange or juice from tinned fruits]

1/2 cup [125 mL] white wine or beer, water to cover

1 tbsp [15 mL] pickling spice

Rinse the tongue. Place in large pot and cover with juices, wine or beer, water and pickling spice. Gently simmer for 7 to 10 hours. Cool. Remove tongue from liquid and devein. Place in a bowl or mold [a large empty cottage cheese container makes a nice mold].

Molding the Tongue

1/2 can consommé soup

2 tbsp [30 mL] sherry

1/2 tbsp [7 mL] gelatin, dissolved in little water

Heat consommé, sherry and dissolved gelatin. Pour over tongue. Cover with a plate and place a weight on top of the plate [to press the tongue firmly into the bowl or mold]. Refrigerate overnight or all day. Unmold and serve with Mustard Sauce. Note: This mold is most attractive made with 2 tongues.

Mustard Sauce

This smooth, gentle sauce is a good accompaniment for cold tongue, cold ham, spiced beef and corned beef.

2 cups [500 mL] brown sugar

2 tbsp [30 mL] flour

1/2 cup [125 mL] dry mustard

1/2 tsp [2 mL] salt

1 cup [250 mL] vinegar

1 cup [250 mL] water

2 beef bouillon cubes

Mix all ingredients together in a heavy saucepan. Simmer for 20 minutes. Cool. Serve with Cold Tongue or Baked Ham.

HORSE RACING AND HUNTING

Ranchers had a passion for horse racing, whether it was an informal race between two cowboys showing off their favourite horses or an organized event with competitors from across the country. Almost every village and town had a racing track of some sort, and there were tracks even where there were no towns. Cowboys, Indians and local ranchers all participated.

The Mitford and Cochrane Annual Race was a full-day affair with twenty-one events. The most prestigious, the Gentleman Ranchers' Race, called for a race of one mile. The requirements were that the horse had been owned by its master at least three months prior to the race and that it had never been ridden in the racing circuit.

A gathering at the Davies ranch, Crawling Valley, Alberta. c. 1909.
Photo credit: Glenbow Archives

Families arrived in buggies, wagons and democrats. Old friends were reunited and everyone talked horses. At noon, tablecloths were spread on the ground and picnic lunches brought out. One glimpsed roast chicken, basins of salad, sausage rolls, meat patties, sandwiches, fudge layer cake, jelly rolls, cookies and doughnuts.

At the turn of the century, ranchers of British origin raised hounds and organized hunts similar to the traditional fox hunts in the old country. Both men and women participated, making quite a sight as they galloped across the prairies after the lowly coyote. As well as providing sport, the hunts helped keep the coyote population in check.

After the fall roundup, many ranchers loaded up pack strings and rode into the hills for a week or two of big game hunting. Mary Dover recalled that her grandfather, a rancher and former colonel in the North-West Mounted Police, always looked forward to a fall hunt in the foothills and always took with him a meat pie, made in a metal wash basin and large enough to provide a meal for several days.[19]

Sausage Rolls

Millarville was named after early settlers, the Malcolm Millars, who ran the first post office in the area. Mrs. Millar frequently made sausage rolls as did many other ranch women in the area. They were part of picnic lunches taken to the Millarville Races.[20]

Rough Puff Pastry

2 cups [500 mL] flour

1/4 tsp [1 mL] salt

3/4 cup [175 mL] butter, very cold and hard [or 1/2 cup/125 mL butter and 1/4 cup/50 mL lard]

3 to 4 tbsp [45 to 60 mL] cold water to mix

1/2 tsp [2 mL] lemon juice

Sausage Meat Filling

Makes approximately 18 two inch [5 cm] rolls or 36 one inch [2.5 cm] rolls

1 pound [500 g] sausage meat

1 small onion, grated [about 2 tbsp or 30 mL]

1 tbsp [15 mL] chopped parsley

salt and pepper to taste

Sift the flour and salt together. Cut in the fat, leaving it in small pieces. Make a well in the centre. Add the lemon juice and just enough of the water to make a stiff dough. Refrigerate about 1 hour before using. Combine the meat filling ingredients.

To assemble the Sausage Rolls, cut the pastry in half. Roll half the pastry into a 9x13 inch [23x33 cm] rectangle. Form one half of the sausage meat into 3 rolls the length of the pastry and place on the pastry, at an equal distance apart. Cut the pastry into strips wide enough to encircle the meat. Dampen one edge of each strip, fold over and press together firmly. Cut into rolls of desired length. Make a slash on top of each roll. Repeat with the other half of the pastry and sausage. Brush the top with a small amount of beaten egg yolk. Place on a baking sheet with a raised edge. Bake in a hot oven [425° F or 220° C] for approximately 20 to 30 minutes.

COME TO THE BRANDING

Many social occasions for ranch people revolve around work, such as roundups and brandings. As many as one hundred people might come to a branding, most of them to help in some way. The hosts are up early to wrangle, saddle and bridle the horses. Work begins early with skilled riders and their cutting horses roping calves and hauling them bawling and protesting to the corrals where they are castrated, earmarked, inoculated and branded. Most of the people work. Those not working sit on the corral rails and enjoy the bustle of animals, people, fires and the outdoors. The women on the ranch have been preparing for this event well ahead of time. Neighbours help by bringing enormous pans of cakes, cookies and pies. Nobody comes empty-handed to a branding.

The noon meal is brought out and served buffet style from the back of a truck bed although a few ranchers still like to keep the old tradition and bring out their chuckwagon on these special occasions. Food is simple: pots of beans, a hearty stew, salads, homemade buns, choice of pie and coffee.

Work continues until all the calves have been branded and the cows dehorned. Cows and calves are turned out on the range and the branding is finished for another year.

Now the visiting and celebrating begins. Prime rib roasts or a hip of beef have been barbecued. An assortment of salads, homemade buns, pies—apple, rhubarb, raisin, saskatoon—are spread out on a long table. Talk turns to cattle and horses and brandings of long ago.

Potluck Bean Supper

Baked beans are a tradition at brandings and other western celebrations. This Baked Bean dish is hearty enough to be served as a main course.

Serves 8

2 pounds [1 kg] ground beef
2 medium onions, chopped
2-28 fl. oz [796 mL] cans beans
2/3 cup [150 mL] brown sugar
1/3 cup [75 mL] vinegar
1 cup [250 mL] ketchup or canned tomatoes
2 tsp [10 mL] dry mustard
2 tsp [10 mL] Worcestershire sauce

Brown the beef. Sauté the onions. Add to beans. Combine remaining ingredients and add to bean mixture. Bake slowly in a 300° F [150° C] oven for 1-2 hours. Time will depend on the type of baking dish used. A heavy bean pot will take up to 2 hours.

Ranch House Stew

If serving this dish to guests, prepare stew ahead of time and have ingredients measured for the biscuit topping. The dish will then take only a few minutes to assemble.

Beef Stew Base

Serves 8 to 10

4 pounds [2 kg] beef rump or stew meat, cut into cubes

4 large onions, chopped

3/4 cup [175 mL] flour

1 tsp [5 mL] paprika

1 cup [250 mL] canned tomatoes

1 glass beer [optional]

2 tsp [10 mL] Worcestershire sauce

4 cups [1 L] brown stock or water with 4 beef bouillon cubes dissolved

3 bay leaves

1 tsp [5 mL] parsley

1/4 tsp [1 mL] thyme

2 cups [500 mL] mushrooms, whole or sliced

1 tsp [5 mL] salt

pepper to taste

Trim fat from meat. Place pieces of fat in a heavy pan to render fat. Discard the dried bits. Brown meat in fat [add lard if there is not enough]. Remove meat and brown onions. Return the meat to the pan. Add flour and paprika. Stir well. Continue cooking for a few minutes. Add the tomatoes, beer, Worcestershire sauce, stock, bay leaves, parsley and thyme. Cover and bake in a 300° F [150° C] oven or simmer on top of stove for 3 hours, until meat is tender. Add mushrooms, salt and pepper.

Pour stew into a 3 quart [3 L] casserole or two smaller casseroles. Prepare the biscuit crust.

Biscuit Crust

2 cups [500 mL] flour

1 tbsp [15 mL] baking powder

1/2 tsp [2 mL] salt

4 tbsp [60 mL] butter

1 egg

3/4 cup [175 mL] milk

Mix dry ingredients. Work in butter until mixture resembles crumbs. Beat egg with the milk. Make a well in centre of dry ingredients; pour in egg and milk and mix until one lump of dough is obtained. Roll out on a floured board to 1/2 inch [1.5 cm] thickness. Cut to fit the size of the casserole. Place the dough over stew in casserole and seal edge tightly to keep flavour in. Brush the top with milk and bake in a 400° F [200° C] oven for approximately 20 minutes or until browned.

THE FIRST OF JULY

In the early 1900s the social event of the year was the community picnic on the first of July. There were horse races and horse-breaking events. The children participated in foot races and jumping contests. Married women competed against single women in thread and needle races. A tug of war pitted the married men against the bachelors. There were wheelbarrow races, egg and spoon races, and pie-eating contests.

After the organized events, the children played games of hide and seek, ante-I-over and ring around the rosy. Teams were chosen for ballgames. Older men threw horseshoes, ladies visited.

Picnickers attending a gymkhana on the Roo Dee Ranch, Pincher Creek, Alberta. Social life centred around sporting occasions: rodeos, brandings, hunts and gymkhanas. c. 1899. Photo credit: Glenbow Archives

Two or three families with icehouses and a summer supply of ice brought ice cream freezers, a block of ice and the makings for ice cream. The men packed the freezers with chipped ice and turned the handles until they would crank no more. They were packed with more ice, covered with a blanket and left until the ice cream hardened.

When it was time for the picnic lunch, tablecloths and blankets were spread under the trees and the homemade specialties were displayed. Everyone filled a plate with cold baked ham, fried chicken, jellied chicken, potato salad, coleslaw, jellied fruit, chutney, beet pickles, buttered buns, fudge layer cake, sponge cake, ginger cake, jelly roll, rhubarb pie, pumpkin pie, cookies and lemonade.

At last the ice cream was unpacked. The thought of its coolness made everyone hurry over with a dish and spoon to stand in line for a taste.

Deviled Eggs

Deviled eggs were part of every picnic lunch.

Serves 8

4 hard-cooked eggs

1 tbsp [15 mL] butter or mayonnaise

2 tbsp [30 mL] grated cheddar cheese

tomato sauce or ketchup to taste

1/2 tsp [2 mL] salt

1/8 tsp [1/2 mL] cayenne pepper

parsley

Shell eggs and cut in half lengthwise. Cut off a piece from the base to allow them to stand firmly. Remove yolks and mix with softened butter, cheese, tomato sauce and seasoning. Sieve or mash the mixture well. Fill egg white with the mixture using a spoon or force through a tube. Place a sprig of parsley or small pieces of green or red pepper on top of each half egg.

Three Bean Salad

Serves 8

14 oz [398 mL] can cut wax beans

14 oz [398 mL] can french-style green beans

14 oz [398 mL] can kidney beans

1 can mushrooms [optional]

1 cup [250 mL] thinly sliced onions

1/2 cup [125 mL] salad oil

1/2 cup [125 mL] dark cider vinegar

3/4 cup [175 mL] sugar

salt and pepper to taste

The day before you plan to serve this salad, combine all beans [well drained] with the sliced onions and mushrooms. Shake oil, vinegar, sugar, salt and pepper in a jar. Pour over the bean mixture. Cover and refrigerate, stirring occasionally.

Just before serving, drain beans and pile on crisp salad greens or toss with an equal portion of greens using a little bit of marinade as a dressing.

CHRISTMAS ON THE RANCH

When it's -32° F outside, the house is snug within, the old weathered logs wrapping the rooms like a warm cocoon. The green boughs of the Christmas tree, strung with threaded cranberries, lend a festive air, while the tissue-wrapped presents heighten the feeling of expectancy.

Vivian Cowan, Onward Ranch, 150 Mile House, British Columbia, wrote: "We always have to wait Christmas morning until the cattle are fed, hundreds of them and of course being so cold it takes longer to do as they get extra then so it's about eleven when Hugh comes in and gives his men a hot rum. He then changes to be ready for the fray. Meanwhile the children are almost bursting with impatience. Finally we all gather."

The presents are opened. Friends drop by. Dinner preparations are made and the smell of turkey permeates the house. The long table is covered with an Irish linen tablecloth, candles and Christmas crackers. A guest or two leavens the family, although everyone is in the best of spirits anyway.

Now the turkey is ready to be carved, the sage stuffing spooned to a waiting bowl and the gravy poured into a jug. The potatoes are whipped, the creamed onions given a pinch of nutmeg and the frozen garden peas a sprinkling of dried mint. Meanwhile jellies and pickles brought up from the cellar are resplendent in their china dishes, and the cut glass bowl filled with cole-slaw is decorated with a sprig of holly. The mince pie is in the warming oven and the Christmas plum pudding awaits its moment of grandeur when it will be carried to the dining room table alight with brandy.

Christmas Day and Christmas week provide an opportunity to slow down, to read a new book, to gather with the family over a jigsaw puzzle and to visit with neighbours.

Weather permitting, it is a time for sleighing, tobogganing, skiing and skating parties. Sometimes there is a big bonfire in the pasture, with mulled wine and hot dogs, followed by coffee, mince tarts and Christmas cake back at the ranch house.[21]

Spiced Beef for the Holiday Season

When the Cowans lived on the Onward Ranch in British Columbia, it was traditional to serve Spiced Beef at an open house during Christmas week. "It always caused a little sensation," recalled Vivian Cowan in her letters to friend Fay Hartt. The original recipe specified a whole round of beef, with the bone removed and the cavity filled with suet, tied up and marinated in spices for three weeks.

Opposite: A happy group enjoying a sleigh ride on Rosebud Creek, Alberta. Photo credit: Glenbow Archives

12 to 14 pounds [6 to 7 kg] rolled round of beef
1 cup [250 mL] brown sugar
1-1/2 cups [375 mL] coarse or pickling salt
3 tbsp [45 mL] allspice
3 tbsp [45 mL] cloves
2 tbsp [30 mL] saltpetre
1/2 cup [125 mL] peppercorns [cracked]

Tie beef with heavy cord to hold the shape. Rub brown sugar into meat on all sides, place meat in a bowl or crock and leave in a cool place for 3 days. Rub meat with sugar liquid and turn once each day. Mix salt, allspice, cloves, saltpetre and peppercorns. Rub into beef and return to the bowl or crock.* Store in a cool place for 2 to 3 weeks. Each day turn meat to opposite side and rub all sides with the collected juices.

* If you do not have a suitable crock, place mari-nated meat in a large ziplock plastic bag [double bag to be sure it won't leak]. Store in the back of the refrigerator and turn every day.

To cook the meat:

Drain meat and wrap tightly in foil. Bake in a 300° F [150° C] oven for approximately 2 - 3 hours. Use a meat thermometer and cook to medium rare or your preference. Cool in juice and store in the refrigerator.

To serve, carve across grain in very thin slices. Serve with two or three varieties of sliced buttered bread, mustard and horseradish.

Tomato Aspic

Tomato Aspic is a good accompaniment for Spiced Beef at winter buffets and makes a refreshing jellied salad for cold suppers.

Serves 4 to 6

14 oz [398 mL] can canned tomatoes

1/2 cup [125 mL] water

3 oz package [85 g] lemon jello powder

1 tbsp [15 mL] vinegar

dash of Worcestershire sauce

Bring tomatoes and water to a boil; stir in remaining ingredients. [Do not break up tomatoes.] Cool slightly and pour into a glass serving bowl. Serve cold.

Cucumbers with Cream

Serves 8 to 10

3 cucumbers, peeled and sliced thin

1 tbsp [15 mL] salt

1 small onion, finely chopped or 3 green onions

1 cup [250 mL] thick cream, sour or sweet

1 tbsp [15 mL] vinegar

2 tbsp [30 mL] sugar

freshly ground pepper to taste

Place cucumbers in a bowl and sprinkle with salt. Set a weight on top of the cucumbers. Refrigerate for several hours, then pour off the juice. Mix onion[s], cream, vinegar, sugar and pepper. Pour over the cucumbers.

Orange Charlotte

Oranges and lemons were a rare treat and any desserts incorporating them were given special rating. One of the recipes was a modified version of the classic dessert Orange Charlotte Russe. It was brought to the table in a beautiful china fruit bowl and spooned into sherbet glasses.

Serves 8

4 tsp [20 mL] unflavoured gelatin

1/3 cup [75 mL] cold water

1/2 cup [125 mL] boiling water

1/2 cup [125 mL] sugar

1/4 cup [50 mL] lemon juice or orange-flavoured liqueur

1 tsp [5 mL] grated orange rind

1 cup [250 mL] orange juice and pulp

3 egg whites

1 cup [250 mL] heavy cream, whipped

Soften the gelatin in cold water, add boiling water and stir until gelatin is dissolved. Add the sugar, lemon juice or liqueur, orange rind and juice. Chill until syrupy. Add egg whites, beaten stiff but not dry. Fold in whipped cream. Pour into a serving bowl, garnish with orange slices. Chill until firm.

Christmas Plum Pudding

A flaming pudding is a spectacular ending to the festive meal. To flame, heat 1/4 cup [50 mL] brandy in a small container. Just before carrying to the table, pour hot brandy over the pudding and set alight.

Serves 10 to 12

1 cup [250 mL] seedless raisins

1 cup [250 mL] sultana raisins

1 cup [250 mL] currants

1/3 cup [75 mL] brandy, rum or fruit juice

1 cup [250 mL] grated carrots

juice and rind of 1 lemon

1/4 cup [50 mL] marmalade or jam

1/4 cup [50 mL] walnuts or pecans [chopped]

1 cup [250 mL] moist brown sugar

1 cup [250 mL] fine bread crumbs

1 cup [250 mL] flour

1 tsp [5 mL] baking soda

1/2 tsp [2 mL] salt

1 tsp [5 mL] cinnamon

1/4 tsp [1 mL] each cloves, nutmeg and mace

3/4 cup [175 mL] butter [or 1 cup suet]

3 eggs, beaten

Wash raisins and currants and place in a large mixing bowl. Add brandy and if time permits allow fruit to soak for several hours or overnight.

Add carrots, lemon, marmalade, nuts, sugar and bread crumbs. Sift flour, soda, salt and spices over the fruit and mix well. Cream butter and beat in eggs one at a time. Stir into raisin flour mixture. Spoon mixture into a well-buttered 8 cup [2 L] bowl or mold, or into 2 smaller molds and cover with foil.

Select a pot or kettle with a lid large enough to hold mold. The mold can be a special pudding mold, a salad bowl, a metal bowl, a Pyrex bowl, quart [litre] sealers or an empty coffee can. It should be no more than 2/3 full of batter. Place a low rack, trivet or wire on the kettle bottom and set the covered mold on rack. Pour enough water into kettle to reach halfway up mold. Cover the kettle and bring water to a boil. Maintain steam for approximately 4 hours.

Check during steaming and add more water if necessary. When pudding is done, remove the foil, cool, and cover with clean, dry foil. Store in a cool place. The pudding will keep for a long time if kept cool and is best if allowed at least two weeks to ripen.

Before serving, steam for 1 hour or wrap in foil and reheat for 1 hour in the oven. Unmold on a serving plate and garnish with a sprig of holly. Serve with Brown Sugar Sauce [Cowboys and Chuckwagons] or Hard Sauce.

To flame, just before serving heat 1/4 cup [50 mL] brandy or rum, light with a match, pour over the pudding and carry to the table.

Hard Sauce

This recipe is less sweet than most hard sauces and is suitable for serving after a heavy dinner.

Serves 6 to 8

1/2 cup [125 mL] butter

1/2 cup [125 mL] fine sugar [berry or icing sugar]

1 tbsp [15 mL] brandy

1 tsp [5 mL] finely grated lemon rind

1/4 tsp [1 mL] grated nutmeg

Cream butter. Add sugar gradually, continuing to beat until the mixture is light and fluffy. Add the brandy and lemon rind. Beat. Spoon into a glass serving bowl. Grate nutmeg over top. Chill thoroughly.

Preserved Ginger Cake

Ginger was frequently used in drinks, cookies and cake. This recipe makes an attractive and delicious cake to serve with tea or coffee at an evening party or afternoon picnic.

3/4 cup [175 mL] butter

1/2 cup [125 mL] white sugar

1/2 cup [125 mL] brown sugar

2 eggs

2 cups [500 mL] all-purpose flour

1 tsp [5 mL] baking soda

1/2 tsp [2 mL] cinnamon

1/2 tsp [2 mL] grated nutmeg

1/2 tsp [2 mL] salt

1 cup [250 mL] sour milk

3/4 cup [175 mL] preserved ginger, chopped

Cream the butter until fluffy, add the sugars and beat until the brown sugar has dissolved. Beat in the eggs, one at a time. Sift together the dry ingredients. Mix them into the creamed mixture alternately with the sour milk. Fold in the preserved ginger. Spoon into a greased and floured 8 inch [20 cm] tube pan. Bake at 350° F [180° C] for 45 to 50 minutes. Turn out and cool. When almost cool, spread Glace Icing over the top and let it dribble down the sides.

Glace Icing

1 cup [250 mL] icing sugar

2 tbsp [30 mL] lemon juice or milk

water to moisten

Mix the ingredients together and spread over the top of the cake.

NOTES

1   Jock Carpenter, *Fifty Dollar Bride* [Gray's Publishing Ltd., Sidney, British Columbia, 1977].

2   Meriel Hayden, in an interview with the author, Longview, Alberta, 1980. A story about her grandmother.

3   Monica Hopkins, Manuscript *Log Cabin and We Two, 1909-10* [Glenbow Archives, Calgary, Alberta], 128.

4   Mrs. J. L. Sexsmith, High River, Alberta, interviewed by E. G. Luxton, 1956 [Glenbow Archives, Calgary, Alberta].

5   Adapted from the personal cookbook of Mrs. Royden [Jean] Fraser. It belonged to her great aunt Mrs. Rose Reider.

6   Printed with the permission of Mrs. Robert [Jean] Fisher. The recipe comes from a handwritten book belonging to her grandmother Mary Stewart.

7   Margaret Ward [pen name of Mary Inderwick], Letters, 1884 [Glenbow Archives, Calgary, Alberta].

8   The Sheppard Family, E. G. Luxton interview with Bert Sheppard, High River, Alberta, 1958 [Glenbow Archives, Calgary, Alberta].

9   Moira O'Neill, "A Lady's Life on a Ranche," *Blackwood's Edinborough Magazine, Vol. 163, 1898* [Glenbow Archives, Calgary, Alberta].

10 Erica Woodward,"The First Batch," in the Co-operative Women's Guild, *The Golden Curtain Rises* [Swift Current, Saskatchewan, 1964], 20. Reproduced by permission of her family.

11 Monica Hopkins, "Log Cabin," 39.

12 Susan Allison, *A Pioneer Gentlewoman in British Columbia,* Ed. Margaret A. Ormsby. Reprinted with permission of the University of British Columbia Press [Vancouver, 1976], 62-64.

13 Annie McKinnon Fuller, in an interview with the author, 1979.

14 Cochrane and Area Historical Society, *Big Hill Country* [Cochrane, Alberta, 1977], 119.

15 Mrs. Kate de Veber, Pioneer Interviews by Edna Kells, c. 1935 [Glenbow Archives, Calgary, Alberta], 9-10.

16 Adapted from a recipe in Katie Moffatt's handwritten cookbook, now in the possession of descendants Mr. and Mrs. William Toole, Calgary, Alberta.

17 *Big Country Cariboo Magazine*, Winter/Spring 1978.

18 Ken Mather, *Home Sweet Home, A History of the Historic O'Keefe Ranch 1867-1977* [O'Keefe Ranch, Vernon, British Columbia, 1995].

19 Mary Dover, in an interview with the author, Okotoks, Alberta, 1977.

20 Mildred McMillan, correspondence with author, 1977.

21 Vivian Cowan, correspondence, Onward Ranch, 150 Mile House [Provincial Archives of British Columbia].

BIBLIOGRAPHY

Allison, Susan, *A Pioneer Gentlewoman in British Columbia*, Ed. Margaret A. Ormsby, Vancouver, British Columbia: University of British Columbia Press, 1976.

Cochrane and Area Historical Society, *Big Hill Country*, Cochrane, Alberta, 1977.

Gould, Jan, *Women of British Columbia*, Saanichton, British Columbia: Hancock House Publishers, 1975.

Mather, Ken, *Home Sweet Home, A History of the Historic O'Keefe Ranch 1867-1977*, Vernon, British Columbia: O'Keefe Ranch, 1995.

Pincher Creek Historical Society, *Prairie Grass to Mountain Pass; History of the Pioneers of Pincher Creek and District*, Calgary, Alberta: D. W. Friesen & Sons Ltd., 1974.

Thomas, Lewis G. Paper, *Ranch Houses of the Alberta Foothills*, Glenbow Archives, Calgary, Alberta, 1974.

Willow Creek Historical Society, *Echoes of Willow Creek*, Lethbridge, Alberta, Lethbridge Herald, 1965.

PHOTO CREDITS

Glenbow Archives, Calgary, Alberta: pages 4, 6, 8, 10, 14, 16, 18, 20, 24, 26, 28, 30, 36, 40, 42

The Historic O'Keefe Ranch, Vernon, British Columbia: page 34

Museum of the Highwood, High River, Alberta: page 12

Provincial Archives of British Columbia, Victoria, British Columbia: page 22

THE AUTHOR

Beulah (Bunny) Barss graduated with a home economics degree from the University of Saskatchewan, qualified as a dietitian at the Royal Victoria Hospital in Montreal and received an M.A. from the University of Calgary. Her interests include preserving the rich heritage of ranching and pioneering experiences, particularly regarding food and cooking. She is the author of *The Pioneer Cook, Come'n Get It; Favorite Ranch Recipes, Oh! Canada*, and co-author of *Prairie Homesteaders* and *Alberta Pictorial Cookbook*.